The "Journey of a Lifetime"
Book One

Don't Be Bitter

Shawnte Kinney

To Bruce Lee,

You let me breathe.
Thanks for helping me find the strength and the courage to find me.

ACKNOWLEDGEMENTS

I want to first give God all the honor that he deserves. He has kept me, preserved me, guided me and restored me. Nothing that I do is without him for he is everything. I would also like to thank my mother. I love you so much and appreciate everything that you have instilled in me. I did not understand so much of it, but you fought for me when every other person walking on this earth could not and for that my gratefulness runs deep. My special girl, Bella, I just love you sweet girl. To my babies, I keep moving for all of you. You guys keep me humble and honest. To my boss and friend, don't know much to say but thank you for everything. To my Pastor and First Lady, I appreciate you both so much. Thank you for being a consistent example. You both are full of so much grace and love and I am honored that God chose you both to shepherd me. To my accountability partners, you ladies are my rock. Thank you for every hug and for listening and encouraging me and your constant and consistent prayers. To Amy, thank you so much for catching the vision and creating the most amazing book cover. To my manifestation partner, girl, our superpowers have been activated. To my girls! We have been through so much and yet all of us are still standing, rooted and grounded in such deep love, respect and appreciation for each other. Life would not be life without each of you unique women. I am blessed beyond measure for all of you. Ladies!!

Prologue

"When you come out of the storm you won't be the same person that walked in. That's what the storm is all about."
-Haruki Murakami

God told me this on January 28, 2014. I didn't get it at the time. I had no clue at that moment when I read this, about the storm that was about to hit my life. A storm that was going to challenge the very foundation of my character. A storm that would change me, change my life, change my thinking, change the way I saw myself. This was all the warning I received and to be honest, I didn't remember this warning until years later. But the storm, just as promised, came. In March 2014 my husband lost his stepmom, in April 2014 he lost his uncle and in September 2014 he suddenly lost his mom. Needless to say, 2015 was not easy for us. Then, on a Sunday afternoon in 2016, my husband of 14 years walked in and told me that I didn't make him happy anymore and that he wanted a divorce.

Of course, one can only imagine the level of devastation and pain that erupted within me. In that moment of pain, I remember walking outside and telling God that this would be an appropriate time for Him to take my life. A real part of me believed that I would pass away in my sleep that night. In my heart, I believed that I had fulfilled my purpose in the lives of those that I had helped throughout the years and it was time. I believed that I had lived a good, full and complete life and had experienced a great love, so in that moment I honestly believed that I was ready for death and so I prayed and with a sincere heart asked God to just allow me to go on to heaven.

I will admit, at that moment I wanted anything to keep me from experiencing the emotional pain and betrayal that I was feeling and that I knew I was about to endure. But God in all His sovereignty denied my request. After spending the next few days crying until I didn't think I had anymore tears left, God simply asked me if I was going to lay there or get up. So, with every ounce of strength I had, I got up. God told me he was about to take me on an unbelievable journey.

What started out as the most heartbreaking moment of my life as I knew it, has turned into the most amazing journey of self-discovery, healing, forgiveness, and love. What follows is a detailed day-by-day, journal of my journey to complete oneness with God, of how He fed me daily in my wilderness, of how He helped me to overcome the pains of bitterness and anger and how I experienced His healing and became enlightened to the real power and love of God. My prayer is that my journey helps you to take whatever moment you may be in and experience the power of God's love and healing as you process and endure your moment of affliction.

The place where you have been happy may soon become
your place of affliction, and that may prove to be your greatest cross.

Don't Be Bitter

Book One

June 28, 2016 – September 12, 2016

June 28, 2016

On Sunday my husband, Gary, of 14 years, told me I didn't make him happy anymore and he wanted a divorce. Let's just say the past few days have not been good for me. Today is Tuesday, but it is also day one, a new beginning. In the middle of my crying, God spoke to me today and told me He wanted me to love like He loves. He told me to journal my days as I take this journey to forgiveness and healing. I will try to be honest about how I feel every day. I am not scared, but I am hurt. However, I know all is going to be well. My prayer today is that God covers Gary's mind and keep him whole.

My manna from Heaven today:

My scripture for today that encouraged me and confirmed that I was on the right path:

Philippians 3:13-14:

Brethren, I count not myself to have apprehended: but this one thing I do, forgetting those things which are behind, and reaching forth unto those things which are before, I press toward the mark for the prize of the high calling of God in Christ Jesus.

Went to Barnes & Noble. This was the journal just sitting there waiting on me. Knew it was God!!

My run at Brookhaven after my 15 minute breakdown. Believe it or not this smile is really real!

June 29, 2016

Woke up today feeling encouraged and positive. I had a long talk with my Pastor last night. He helped to try to explain things from Gary's point of view. I am praying that God will help me to see things with different eyes. I do know that all decisions are left to me. I believe that God will honor whatever direction I choose and whatever road I decide to take. I thank Him for giving me a choice. Currently in my life, it feels as though others are constantly trying to take my choices away from me. I went and checked out ILovekickboxing today. Figured it was time to try something new.

"

Whatever you vividly imagine,
ardently desire, sincerely believe, and
enthusiastically act upon must
inevitably come to pass!

Paul J. Meyer

My manna from Heaven today:

Psalm 138:8 The LORD will perfect that which concerneth me: thy mercy, O LORD, endureth forever: forsake not the works of thine own hands.

This scripture blessed me so much today!!

This was right on time today.

God gives me what I need for every day.

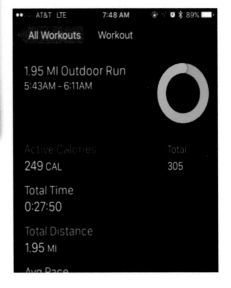

Had to go work out today to clear my head.

June 30, 2016

I understand that every day of this journey is not going to be a good day, but each day that I wake up and I am not angry or bitter, I am going to consider that a win. I have been listening to Sheryl Brady talking about loving people on another level. I don't know that I am in a place to love the way Hosea loved Gomer. I may have not matured to that level yet. My dog Bella was sick this morning. I realized that you must be thankful for the small things. Gary and I are not communicating well right now, but we did come together in concern about her. My prayer is that the both of us learn to be grateful for all things and that the Lord will help our understanding.

"

Do a little more each day than you think you possibly can.

Lowell Thomas

My manna from heaven today. Thank You Lord!!!

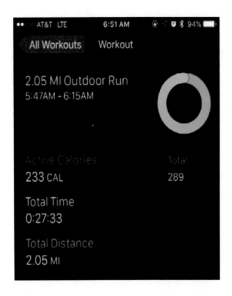

Hannah Whitall Smith: Confidence is not based on wishful thinking but in knowing that God is in control.

Scripture: Romans 8:28 And we know that all things work together for good to them that love God, to them who are the called according to his purpose.

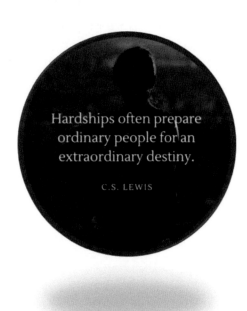

Hardships often prepare ordinary people for an extraordinary destiny.

C.S. LEWIS

July 1, 2016

This is going to sound crazy, but even with all that is going on, I LOVE MY LIFE!!! I credit it all to my relationship with God. God speaks, I listen and do what he says. It is very fulfilling, especially knowing I am not by myself. Today God talked to me on seeds and roots and He showed me some things. I thank God for the root in my own life. I did text Gary to say let's not let our pride ruin us and suggested that we both look at ourselves and then really talk. However, he didn't respond back. My prayer, that the spirit of pride will not destroy us or what we have built.

"

You see, in life, lots of people know what to do, but few people actually do what they know. Knowing is not enough! You must take action.

Tony Robbins

My manna from Heaven today:

Psalm 118:24 This is the day which the LORD hath made; we will rejoice and be glad in it.

Romans 12:3: For I say, through the grace given unto me, to every man that is among you, not to think of himself more highly than he ought to think; but to think soberly, according as God hath dealt to every man the measure of faith.

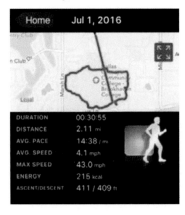

Resolve to make every day count. Be a woman of action. Treat each day as precious.
Emilie Barnes

July 2, 2016

The last week has been absolutely amazing. All things work together for the good of those that love the Lord. God is not only loving me, but he is teaching me. Seeing through new eyes. Watch what he gives. All my manna today lined up about time. I went and treated myself at the spa last night; really relaxing and nice. Yesterday I was informed I was getting a 10% raise!! Snooping, I did find out Gary has been looking at apartments. That was painful to find, but yet, I am still full of joy. I am learning to enjoy myself. I look around and see plenty of life. It goes on even when your life isn't perfect. Today's prayer: Lord help me to humble myself and know my value. Don't allow me to settle.

> **"**
>
> *There's no next time. It's now or never.*
>
> **Celestine Chua**

My manna from heaven today:

I don't really want more time; I just want enough time. Time to breathe deep and time to see real and time to laugh long, time to give You glory and rest deep and sing joy.

Ann Voskamp

But I trusted in thee, O LORD: I said, Thou art my God. My times are in thy hand: deliver me from the hand of mine enemies, and from them that persecute me. Psalm 31:14-15

July 3, 2016

Today is bordering on one of the bad days. Gary came home at 2:30 this morning. That really was not my problem, it is the way he continues to act as though things are normal. That was my breaking point. I couldn't sleep so I was up cleaning, as I got more upset, I woke him up at 4:00 a.m. I needed to talk and he had been avoiding me. A person can only take so much. I may have went off a little bit. But he actually told me he didn't owe me anything and our vows didn't mean anything to him. I told *that spirit* in him "you gotta get out of here. You are no longer welcome." His response, "I don't have anywhere to go." This has been a hard one. My prayer: That I will always recognize my value.

"

The only person you are destined to become is the person you decide to be.

Ralph Waldo Emerson

My manna from Heaven today:

Psalm 16:11: You make known to me the path of life; you will fill me with joy in your presence, with eternal pleasures at your right hand.

GOD IS NOT PUNISHING YOU, HE IS PREPARING YOU. TRUST HIS PLAN NOT YOUR PAIN.

GOD HAS A PURPOSE FOR YOUR PAIN, A REASON FOR YOUR STRUGGLES AND A REWARD FOR YOUR FAITHFULNESS DON'T GIVE UP!

Couldn't stay home had to get out so I went to my cousin's annual 4th of July Bash. Me hanging with family. I have to keep moving.

Me and Serratia.
Sometimes you have to
smile thru it.

Me and my Zoey.
Can't help but smile
in her presence.

July 4, 2016

Sometimes it feels like the twilight zone. After Saturday night/Sunday morning Gary came home at 9:00 p.m. business as usual. God did tell me though now "love him to death." So I put a card in his car letting him know God loves him and I do too. Don't know how he will respond, if he does. Still not going to stop me. He did call me later to tell me who he was with and where he was going plus tried laughing with me and said he was putting rent money in the account, I wasn't expecting that. Love him until completion. But more importantly, loose him and bring him to me. God's word to me today. Prayer: Lord help me to love purely and help him to receive it with clear eyes and pure heart.

It's not what you know, it's what you do with what you know.

Unknown

My manna from Heaven today:

I was made for more than being stuck in a vicious cycle of defeat. I am not made to be a victim of my poor choices. I was made to be a victorious child of God. *Lysa TerKeurst*

When all else fail, meal prep!! Lol.

With God we will gain the victory. Through God we shall do valiantly: for He it is that shall tread down our enemies. Psalm 60:12

July 5, 2016

Okay, so today is a bad day. I laid in bed and cried most of the day feeling sorry for myself. I have to be careful who I talk to also, not everyone understands where I am mentally or spiritually. There is just too much stuff going on in my head. I have been trying to remember when we were a team. It seems so long ago. I don't understand God's plan at times. *Loose him and bring him to me.* He had me make Gary breakfast and give him loving and encouraging words. It broke me to do it, because I am giving him what I need, but I did it nonetheless. I put oil in his food and prayed over it. My prayer today: Lord strengthen me!!.

"

Life is a song - sing it. Life is a game - play it. Life is a challenge - meet it. Life is a dream - realize it. Life is a sacrifice - offer it. Life is love - enjoy it.

Sai Baba

My manna from Heaven today got me out of bed..Yep a lot more than normal!!!

Let people miss you. Sometimes they take you for granted because they think you will always be available. Nope. Miss me when I'm gone.

God and a good wife are the two best things a man can have.

Stay Busy! If you keep your grind right. It will keep your mind right!

July 6, 2016

Today is much better. I have been processing things and I see things better and clearer. The enemy is after my husband, but he can't have him. Some spirts come out by nothing but prayer and fasting. I keep giving him to God. 1 Corinthians 13:4-8 is what God told me to send him today. Have no clue if he even looked at what I sent. I do know he has locked me out of his car. ☺ I did decide to give him until August 1st, to make some type of decision. Prayer: That he remembers or sees what love looks like.

My manna from Heaven today:

Man, God gives me good stuff every single day!!

Psalm 56:11-13: In God have I put my trust: I will not be afraid what man can do unto me. Thy vows are upon me, O God: I will render praises unto thee. For thou hast delivered my soul from death: wilt not thou deliver my feet from falling, that I may walk before God in the light of the living?

> **Isaiah 41:10 (NIV) Do not fear, for I am with you; do not be dismayed, for I am your God. I will strengthen you and help you; I will uphold you with my righteous right hand.**

66

You can't stop the waves, but you can learn to surf.

Anonymous

July 7, 2016

Today was a pretty good day. Worked out this morning. I am clear headed, excited and focused. I say too often I am living in the twilight zone. My husband is a crazy man right now, but God has shown me the generational curses and destruction in his family. I am seeing what I never saw before, he has real problems with commitment. Anytime anything gets hard or is not benefitting him, he cuts and run. My prayer today is that God will break the generational barriers and limitations over him.

"

Anyone who stops learning is old, whether at twenty or eighty. Anyone who keeps learning stays young. The greatest thing in life is to keep your mind young.

Henry Ford

My manna from Heaven today:

Zechariah 4:6 Then he answered and spake unto me, saying, This, is the word of the LORD unto Zerubbabel, saying, Not by might, nor by power, but by my spirit, saith the LORD of hosts.

Yep! Had my first kickboxing class today during lunch this was me trying to get back up off the floor. It was brutal but it was great.

July 8, 2016

Woke up sore as a bug but feeling so good. So much tragedy and senseless death around and still I realize life goes on. Your problems are still there. Looking forward to this weekend stay-vaction. Hate to leave my dog. I haven't been wearing my wedding ring. It was wasn't intentional, I just don't know if I want to put it back on. I didn't work out today, I was so sleepy.

And whatsoever ye do, do it heartily, as to the Lord, and not unto men.
Colossians 3:23

My manna from Heaven today:

Isaiah 58:10-11 and if you spend yourselves in behalf of the hungry and satisfy the needs of the oppressed, then your light will rise in the darkness, and your night will become like the noonday. The LORD will guide you always; he will satisfy your needs in a sun-scorched land and will strengthen your frame. You will be like a well-watered garden, like a spring whose waters never fail.

When I stand before God at the end of my life, I would hope that I would not have a single bit of talent left, and could say, *"I used everything you gave me."* Erma Bombeck

Help me God to use every bit of what you give me every day!

The start of my staycation with Nicole, Carla and Tacha. Oh yes, I am feeling myself!!

July 9, 2016

Started the first day of my mini vacation yesterday. Enjoyed the girls, but this confirmed that I can't drink while I am going through. I started crying in the middle of the club. How pathetic is that!! I am supposed to be happy because I have a husband who wants me so I should be enjoying myself, instead I am looking around because the possibility is strong he may show up with someone. When I wasn't feeling that I felt so alone in the middle of so many people. Anyway, that was yesterday. I am going to enjoy my day today. I did text him to let him know he was on my mind. NO RESPONSE!!!

"

Never give up on something that you can't go a day without thinking about.

Unknown

My Manna from Heaven today…all right what I needed

Colossians 2:6-7 As ye have therefore received Christ Jesus the Lord, so walk ye in him:Rooted and built up in him, and stablished in the faith, as ye have been taught, abounding therein with thanksgiving.

.

He is on my mind at least once every day good and bad. I wonder how often I cross his mind, if at all. But I am on God's mind every day. Now that is encouraging!
Shawnte

Where the focus goes the power flows!!! Praise your way through it to get it out of you. *Sheryl Brady*

24

July 10, 2016

God's grace is so sufficient it can't even be explained. Had a really great weekend. Getting out of my box and not dwelling on all the things going wrong in my life helped. The Word today, God's Got Me Covered. I really wish Gary could come get the Word, it would really help him. But he has to get there by himself. I have to keep lifting him up. I have no clue where he spent the weekend. I am not going to lie and say I don't want to know, because I do. My prayer today is that we will be humble and know we can do nothing without God.

"

If you want to lift yourself up, lift up someone else.

Booker T. Washington

My Manna from Heaven:

Romans 5:5 And hope maketh not ashamed; because the love of God is shed abroad in our hearts by the Holy Ghost which is given unto us.

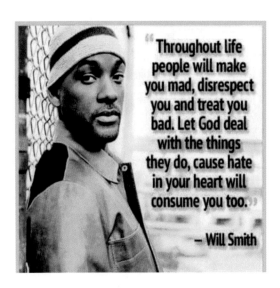

"Throughout life people will make you mad, disrespect you and treat you bad. Let God deal with the things they do, cause hate in your heart will consume you too."

— Will Smith

Even when you don't feel like it.
God to Shawnte

July 11, 2016

Today's word is so interesting. God is right on time to give me everything that I need. Started my fast today from books and any self-pleasure. I am getting ready for our church youth conference. Working hard to keep myself busy and mind focused. Gary is starting to talk more. He thanked me for breakfast today. I prayed over all that food as I was preparing it. God, I need you to really save my husband. Deliver him from himself. Don't let him be lost, but Lord show him You.

"

You must take action now that will move you towards your goals. Develop a sense of urgency in your life.

Les Brown

My Manna from Heaven:
Psalm 55:22 Cast thy burden upon the LORD, and he shall sustain thee: he shall never suffer the righteous to be moved.

Good way to start the week. Getting

in position and staying focused.

God to Shawnte

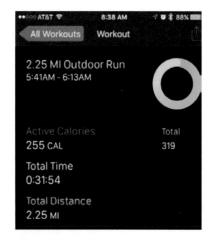

Each day's duties were done
as each day brought them, and
the rest was left with God.
Mary Slessor

July 12, 2016

Life is so full of new stuff and challenges everyday. It is almost impossible to believe that there are people that don't look forward to each new day. You literally have to show up and see what you are going to get each day then use it to the fullest. Wonderful workout this morning. Setting new goals then striving to achieve them. Gary was talkative this morning. I really am confused. This is really what giving him to God looks like. My prayer today is that God will help me to stay righteous and thankful through it all.

My manna from heaven today:

Romans 15:13 May the God of hope fill you with all joy
and peace as you trust in him, so that you may
overflow with hope by the power of the Holy Spirit.
(NIV)

My workout inspiration!!

July 13, 2016

Was laid up in the bed sick all day today. Plenty of time to think
and reflect, mixed with hormones and I promise it wasn't good.
Talked to my dog a lot, yes she is looking at me crazy. Just when
I am at my lowest because I am remembering how he used to
ask me if I was good and needed anything, he calls to see if he
can get me something. My head hurts. I can't stand this!!!!
HELP ME LORD!!!!

"

*The best makeup is a smile. The best
jewelry is modesty. The best clothing is
confidence.*

Unknown

My manna from heaven today:

Our days are in God's hands. He is all-sufficient to meet our needs, and the Savior is with us every step of the way.
Elizabeth George

Somethings have to end so better things can begin. It's not the end of your life, just the end of a chapter. Don't lose yourself. #RehabTime

July 14, 2016

Today's thought: In the past, anytime Gary came across my mind (which was daily), just the thought of him, no matter what, made me smile. Now thoughts of him bring me nothing but sadness and tears and I really hate it. I think that is why God told me to start looking at old pictures of us and I am even sending him pictures. I need to remember. He needs to remember. I don't know if I want to, but I am going to do it. I really need to get to a kickboxing class. This is why working out is so important.

> "
> *A diamond is a piece of charcoal that handled stress exceptionally well.*
>
> Unknown

My manna from heaven today:

Psalm 138:8 The Lord will work out his plans for my life for your faithful love, O Lord, endures forever.

It was real and what God gave me was pure and holy and beautiful. He will give it to me again because I am His child. *Shawnte*

My pain matters. Lord teach me how to trust You even in the middle of it. But please do not allow it to overtake me.
Shawnte

34

July 15, 2016

I really needed my manna today. I can't shake this sadness at all. I just can't seem to reconcile in my heart who this man is that comes in, crushes my life then goes on as if everything is okay and normal. He went from not talking to me at all to now, talking to me about his job, his uncle and other crazy stuff. I, on the inside am raging and confused. I hurt. I am crushed. You don't do that to people that you love. It is so cruel. And I have to look at him every day and sleep in the same sexless bed with him. Lord help me, what do I do? I don't want to move outside of you!!

"

Happiness comes of the capacity to feel deeply, to enjoy simply, to think freely, to risk life, to be needed.

Storm Jameson

My manna from heaven today:

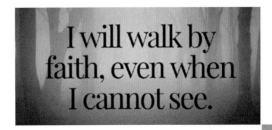

I will walk by faith, even when I cannot see.

You can't change how people feel about you, so don't try. Just live your life and be happy.

January 2012

The cheerful heart has a continual feast.

Proverbs 15:15

July 16, 2016

Man!!! Today this lady felt something. Last night was relationship class (no, Gary didn't show up again). Anyway, I told my First Lady before class I was leaving August 1st. During class I started reading the scriptures and while he can go, I can't. It kinda had me upset with God, but then God reminded me of a few things. First, this that I am going through is not about me. It's all about God's glory. Second, He sits high and looks low. He sees everything I am going through. All is going to be well.

"

Our greatest glory is not in never falling but in rising every time we fall.

Confucius

My manna from heaven today:

For by Thee I have run through a troop; and by my God have
I leaped over a wall.

Psalm 18:29

Our walk-a-thon was
this morning. I
reached my six-mile

July 17, 2016

Today's sermon talked about different levels. 3 Dimensional Me!! Moving to another level. That's why things are looking crazy. I have been encouraged again in my spirit. God is so good. Gary is talking more, about nothing, but more. I don't trust it unfortunately, but I am going with the flow. He was home super early for a Saturday laying across the bed wanting to talk. Life is crazy, but I purposefully am finding reasons to be grateful.

"

Do what you can, with what you have, where you are.

Theodore Roosevelt

My manna from heaven today:

But they that wait upon the LORD shall renew their strength; they shall mount up with wings as eagles; they shall run, and not be weary; and they shall walk, and not faint. Isaiah 40:31

Growing

When you are transitioning to a new season of life, the people and situations that no longer fit you will fall away.

Don't fight
the process

How to make your days better:

If it feels wrong, don't do it.
Say "exactly" what you mean.
Don't be a people pleaser.
Trust your instincts.
Never speak bad about yourself.
Never give up on your dream.
Don't be afraid to say "No".
Be kind to yourself.
Let go of what you can't control.
Stay away from drama and negativity.

July 18, 2016

I woke up this morning feeling some type of way. I wish I could see more clearly. I know things are going to turn out ok, but right now Gary and I are so turned around it is scary. I have decided to just go out and find a couples therapist and set the appointment, and if he comes, he comes. My plan is to find a man who will think like him and help me to see things his way. The therapist needs to be the hardest on me. All I do in life is give up pieces of me so others can be happy. Is that ministry?

My manna from heaven today:

The LORD is my strength and my shield;
my heart trusted in him, and I am helped:
therefore my heart greatly rejoiceth; and
with my song will I praise him. Psalm 28:7

Sometimes I feel like I have to give up too much. Holding on to my imagination is even a challenge.

iWish 25m ago
Athletes visualize winning 1000s of times before they step on the track. They've already won. Other people just don't know it yet....

iWish 25m ago
Imagination is everything. It is the preview of life's coming attractions.

Albert Einstein

iWish 25m ago
You must be the change you want to see in the world.

M.K. Gandhi

July 19, 2016

I realized yesterday, working out is essential in this journey to keep my mind calm. My body is sore, but mind is clear. Having too many thoughts running through my mind is not always good. I found a couples therapist yesterday and set an appointment for this Wednesday. I told Gary. He hasn't said whether he was coming or not, so we will see. I did get a kickboxing class in this morning. I had to, this place of no communication that me and Gary are in felt as if it was destroying me. But now I am feeling good and positive.

"

If you do what you've always done,
you'll get what you've always gotten.

Tony Robbins

My manna from heaven today:

He makes my feet of a deer; he causes me to stand on the heights.
He trains my hands for battle; my arms can bend a bow of bronze.
Psalm 18:33-34

Tracking progress. Top- July 2016; bottom left
August 2015; bottom right April 2016. This year
is all about becoming consistent in my
workouts.

Our first 5K together. September 2013
Richardson, Texas

44

July 20, 2016

What I know today that I didn't know yesterday: pain will force a response. You are going to react to the pain you are feeling, whatever that pain is and in whatever form it comes in. I understand now it is totally up to me how I respond. Emotional pain has got to be the worst. There is no expiration on when it will stop and no medicine to take. You have to learn to breathe through it. Tonight is our counseling session, my mind is working overtime. I want better. I want my abundant life and I wish I could, but I can't accept anything less. Accomplishing goals is all I am focused on right now and it feels good.

"

Always bear in mind that your own
resolution to succeed is more
important than any other.

Abraham Lincoln

My manna from heaven today:

For the Lord God is a sun and shield; the Lord gives grace and glory no good thing does He withhold from those who walk uprightly. Psalm 84:11

I can be changed by
what happens to me.
But I refuse to
be reduced by it.

— Maya Angelou

July 2014 Reunion Tower

Total Time 0:32:53	
Total Distance 2.27 MI	
Avg Pace 14'26" MI	Close
Mile 1	9'30"
Mile 2	16'54"
Mile 3	23'23"

Ran a great mile today..happy dance!!!

Who can be unhappy when you have this face to look at every day. My Bella!!

46

July 21, 2016

I must admit that statement has never been more true in my life than it has been today. Late yesterday Gary told me he was not going to couples counseling. That totally devasted me. Why? Because I was infused with hope. I think I cried for an hour straight. I initially was not going to go but then decided to go by myself. After bible study I put on my worship music and worshipped all the way to counseling. Needless to say, God met me there and I received so many answers and the manna that I needed at that moment. The therapist immediately got it. I asked God to help me to see through new eyes and He gave me new sight. The rest of today totally sucked. My boss lost his mom; Aunt Doris went into the hospital and Uncle Willie was moved to ICU. But even through all of that, I can't help but to feel joy.

My manna from heaven today:

"

*Definiteness of purpose is the starting
point of all achievement.*

W. Clement Stone

DAVID PICKUP, LMFT
16135 PRESTON ROAD
DALLAS, TEXAS 75248
(888) 288-2071

"

*The purpose of life is to live it, to taste
experience to the utmost, to reach out
eagerly and without fear for newer
and richer experience.*

Eleanor Roosevelt

"

*The trick is to enjoy life. Don't wish
away your days, waiting for better
ones ahead.*

Marjorie Pay Hinckley

July 22, 2016

Yesterday was such a long day. Sickness and death is all around me, but trusting and knowing that God is in total control is an amazing thing. Gary is acting almost like his normal self. I am really asking God for a way to get him into counseling, especially with what's going on with his aunt and uncle. As for me, exercising has truly helped keep me sane. Worship is also essential to my mental and overall health. How anyone can live life without worship is beyond me.

"

A man is but of product of his thought,
What he thinks he becomes.

Mahatma Gandhi

My manna from heaven today:

Galatians 6:9: And let us not be weary in well doing: for in due season we shall reap, if we faint not.

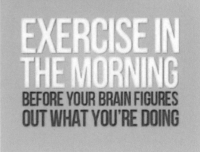

Very proud of myself. Great finish to an otherwise stressful week.

July 23, 2016

My life is crazy. I spent the day at the hospital. I have all sorts of feelings about Gary, but I am choosing to keep going and with everything within me, to stay right and in position. Gary spent the night at a friend's house last night. I am not sure I believe that anymore. But in all things, I will give thanks. Spent the afternoon with Nicole, helping her take her mind off her father who is also dying.

"

If you're not willing to risk, you cannot grow. If you cannot grow, you cannot be your best. If you cannot be your best, you cannot be happy. If you cannot be happy, what else is there?

Les Brown

My manna from heaven today:

I CAN DO ALL THINGS THROUGH CHRIST WHICH STRENGTHENS ME!

Philippians 4:13

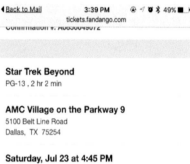

Confirmation #: A065004507Z

Star Trek Beyond
PG-13 , 2 hr 2 min

AMC Village on the Parkway 9
5100 Belt Line Road
Dallas, TX 75254

Saturday, Jul 23 at 4:45 PM
Seats: H3, H4
Auditorium 6

Invite Friends

In the blink of an eye, everything can change. So forgive often and love with all your heart. You may never know when you may not have that chance again.

July 24, 2016

Today, I am totally feeling something. I don't know if I am mad, sad, or hurt but I am tired. Gary didn't come home last night again. He called, said he had to get a drink and wasn't coming home. Crazy how the very thing killing his uncle is what he is using as comfort. The man I married has become a shell of himself. I understand and see things differently today. I have resolved that there is nothing I can do for Gary. Now everything is about keeping my sanity, because watching him self-destruct is not good for me. We are going to have to talk and I am giving him until August 1st to move out.

"

Being realistic is the most commonly traveled road to mediocrity.

Will Smith

My manna from heaven today:

When you realize
God's purpose
for your life isn't
just about you,
He will use you
in a mighty way.

- Dr. Tony Evans

Ephesians 3:16-18 (NIV)
I pray that out of his glorious riches he may strengthen you with power through his Spirit in your inner being, so that Christ may dwell in your hearts through faith. And I pray that you, being rooted and established in love, may have power, together with all the Lord's holy people, to grasp how wide and long and high and deep is the love of Christ.

July 25, 2016

All day yesterday I asked God for strength and courage to have this talk. I asked that He help me to be gentle. God is so wonderful. He told me to be meek, and I was. I at least got a real reaction from Gary which did make things better, it gave me a little hope. Of course, according to him, the problem is me. I am "all over the place" he said, which may be true. But I didn't get upset or even argue. I understand a little better what is going on in his mind. We did have sex, something we haven't done in over two months. All sorts of emotions are running through me, I am certainly feeling overwhelmed. I am praying that God keeps me.

My manna from heaven today:

Joshua 1:9
Have I not commanded you? Be strong and courageous. Do not be afraid; do not be discouraged, for the Lord your God will be with you where you go.

"

**The man who removes a mountain
begins by carrying away small stones.**

Chinese Proverb

July 26, 2016

I am exhausted. Life is beating the living crap out of me and this stuff isn't even about me. Once again, I have all sorts of conflicting feelings toward Gary. His uncle is dying and his aunt is dying, his head is all messed up. He wants to quit his job. He is trying to figure everything out on his own. If things hadn't been going the way they have been between us for the past seven months, I would probably be in a different place toward him mentally, but, it is what it is. I am really trying to be there for everyone and stay in the right mind and spirit, but it isn't easy.

My manna from heaven today:

I didn't focus on any of my Manna today which is why today was a bad day for me. This helped me to see that without what God gives me daily, I can't make it. I don't even want to try!!!

July 27, 2016

Lord, I thank you for your strength and mercy. I am worn out with all this death, pain, stress, problems, attitudes and everything around me, but I am encouraged. Gary's aunt is not doing good at all, she is on life support. His uncle is headed to hospice. My mama is in foreclosure. Someone stole all my money out of my bank account yesterday; and on top of all of that, I am spearheading our youth conference this week. I will admit, yesterday, I wanted a drink so bad. It's a lot. But, I choose to stay encouraged. I am alive. It could be so much worse.

My manna from heaven today:

Psalm 13:6
I will sing to the Lord, because he has dealt bountifully with me.

> Strength, rest, guidance, grace, help, sympathy, love — all from God to us! What a list of blessings.
> Evelyn Stenbock

The big secret in life is that there is no big secret. Whatever your goal, you can get there if you're willing to work.

Oprah Winfrey

July 28, 2016

The Youth Conference is almost over. It has been a very long week. Aunt Doris is doing better. Unfortunately, Uncle Willie isn't. Life is crazy, I promise. The only thing I can do is hang on for the ride and stay grateful.

My manna from heaven today:

2 Corinthians 12:9
And he said unto me, My grace is sufficient for thee: for my strength is made perfect in weakness. Most gladly therefore will I rather glory in my infirmities, that the power of Christ may rest upon me.

July 29, 2016

Woke up extremely exhausted this morning. A lot is going on. Seems like I am always on the go. Moving and not paying attention, I hit a car this morning that was parked behind me. I should have seen the car, but I didn't. My mind was all over the place. I had to take a moment, because all I wanted to do was cry like a baby. But my God is able, and in Him I have so much strength. In the middle of feeling sorry for myself and being overwhelmed, I sit at this funeral and give thanks because that could be me. Thank you Lord for your grace and strength.

My manna from heaven today:

But now thus saith the LORD that created thee, O Jacob, and he that formed thee, O Israel, Fear not: for I have redeemed thee, I have called thee by thy name; thou art mine. When thou passest through the waters, I will be with thee; and through the rivers, they shall not overflow thee: when thou walkest through the fire, thou shalt not be burned; neither shall the flame kindle upon thee. Isaiah 43:1-2

As the chaos swirls and life's demands pull at me on all sides, I will breathe in God's peace that surpasses all understanding. He has promised that He would set within me a peace too deeply planted to be affected by unexpected or exhausting demands. Wendy Moore

"If you really know what you want out of life, it's amazing how opportunities will come to enable you to carry them out." Dr. Goddard

July 30, 2016

We closed out the Youth Conference last night. Man!!! Such an
amazing conference. The kids had such a wonderful time. They
didn't want to leave. Last night filled me with so much strength.
Today our church hosted a community peace walk. So much
unity and strength. So much hope and love. It was great. I am
tired but it was so worth it. Only what I do for Christ will last.
It is a blessing to be used by God.

O Lord, thou hast heard the desire of the
humble: thou wilt prepare their heart, thou wilt
cause thine ear to hear. Psalm 10:17

My manna from Heaven today:

NBCM 2016 Peace Walk (West Dallas, Texas)

July 31, 2016

I rested last night. Gary, who has been gone for the last few days at the hospital, finally came home. We hung out and watched TV. I don't know what God is doing with us, but I am standing still and watching the salvation of the Lord. My sweet girl Bella has been missing me. Always glad to spend time with my favorite girl.

My manna from Heaven today:

A WOMAN who walks in PURPOSE doesn't have to chase PEOPLE or OPPORTUNITIES. Her LIGHT causes PEOPLE and OPPORTUNITIES to PURSUE her.

Two are better than one, because they
have a good return for their work: If one
falls down, his friend can help him up.
Ecclesiastes 4:9-10

August 1, 2016

Back to the twilight zone. Not really, but things are crazy with Gary. I have no idea how to reach him in this place that he has placed himself in. I really don't understand why he would close himself off from me. I have always been in his corner supporting him, encouraging him. But now it is as if he doesn't see me and I am the enemy. I am so tired!!! I have been wondering, do I even want to do this anymore? I know he is worth fighting for, but I don't know that I want to anymore or even for our relationship. I am tired!!! How can a person be full and empty at the same time.

> "
> It is confidence in our bodies, minds and spirits that allows us to keep looking for new adventures, new directions to grow in, and new lessons to learn - which is what life is all about.
>
> Oprah Winfrey

My manna from Heaven today:

Your right hand has held me up, Your gentleness has made me great. Psalm 18:35 NKJV

I know you are tired.
I know you are physically
and emotionally drained.
But you have to keep going.

When a woman feels truly loved, she is confident in herself, she is more generous of heart to be able to reach others, and her faith grows strong because of the deep acceptance she receives and lives in from her Creator.
Sally Clarkson

August 2, 2016

Today has been a quiet day. My sister Nicole lost her father yesterday, so she is not doing good. Gary went back to work today. I am asking God to really help me where he is concerned. I have not exercised in almost two weeks and I am feeling it. Working out is essential to my life and I have got to get back to it. I have also been stress eating. I just need to focus and do better.

66

Those at the top of the mountain didn't fall there.

Marcus Washling

My manna from Heaven today:

Seek the Lord and his strength; seek his face continually. 1 Chronicles 16:11

Learning how to continue to move when my soul hurts so bad is the hardest thing ever. The world doesn't stop because I am in pain or because the man I love doesn't want me anymore. But I have to find a way to keep moving.

Shawnte to herself

August 3, 2016

Today is our anniversary. Can't say that it is a happy one. Uncle Willie died this morning at 4:30. I wish I could describe how I feel today, but this feeling is so alien to me. Gary barely even acknowledged our anniversary or me. I understand to an extent. I really do. But that still stung. How am I supposed to feel? The past year has been true torture. And again, I really had hope that our anniversary would be a moment of reflection and celebration and change things between us. I just wonder in the midst of all of this, when are my concerns going get to any attention? I just want to cry.

My manna from Heaven today:

I couldn't find words to describe what I was feeling then I saw this and it spoke for me. Today is one of the bad days. Tomorrow will be better. This isn't reality, is what God keeps telling me. This is temporary. Don't allow yourself to stay stuck here.

I don't regret our late nights

Talking about the world

And all its problems

I don't regret loving you

Or letting you in

I regret letting you take control

Of me

And my mind

Making me believe

That after all the laughs, tears, and smiles

That what I am

Is not good enough

m.e.

August 4, 2016

Well last night was a breaking point, is the only way to describe it. I had too many glasses of wine and I sat in the middle of the restaurant with Nicole and cried my heart out. But what I find very interesting is how God didn't leave me in the middle of it. He just talked to me the whole time. I heard his voice while I drank wine and cried my soul free. He encouraged me and loved me through my moment of brokenness. There are moments that I feel so special. I never have to wonder if God loves me or if He will answer. He talks to me all the time. I love it!!

My manna from Heaven today:

August 3, 2015 anniversary collage.

This is my reality. God refuses to allow me to forget it and I thank him because even when I can't remember, he does. Happier days are coming.

August 5, 2016

Feeling much better today. I still have not made time to exercise in over two weeks, but I am getting back on it. I have a small vacation coming up and I am looking forward to it. I really need the down time. I just need to remind myself that I matter and my feelings matter. I need to refocus my energy.

My manna from Heaven today:

> "
> *The starting point of all achievement is desire.*
>
> *Napolean Hill*

I can do all things through Christ. Nothing is too hard with God. I can rest if I need to, but I can't quit!!! Me to myself

---

August 6, 2016

I was asleep, and I hear the Spirit of God say in my sleep to get up. When I wake I notice it is 1:30 a.m., and looking around, become aware that once again my husband hasn't come home. I start to get down and angry, but then I start listening to Bishop T.D. Jakes and I immediately understand why God has called me to Him this early in the morning. I cannot control what I will not confront. Loyalty has got to be a guide. That is hard when Gary is working really hard to push me away. I find my comfort and strength in God and in the wisdom that this is not my normal reality. I am fighting generational curses, but my God is greater than anything. I know what I am going through is not going to kill me. Some moments it feels like it will, but God keeps sustaining me. Stand still and watch the salvation of God.

"

Limitations live only in our minds.
But if we use our imaginations, our
possibilities become limitless.

Jamie Paolinetti

My manna from Heaven today:

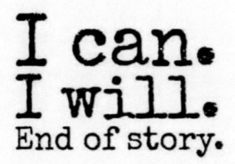

"Be patient everything is coming
together."
@InstaGodMinistries

– God

August 7, 2016

And so, today is one of "those" days. But I am going to rejoice in the Lord and keep moving. God is my strength and courage, even with my broken heart. This pain is really deep. I don't know that I have ever experienced anything so painful but I am reminded that "It is Well!!" One of these days it won't be like this. One of these days my heart will be overflowing with love and joy. I'm so full, yet so empty.

SHOUT OUT TO THOSE

HAVING A HARD TIME

RIGHT NOW.

REMEMBER,

this is only temporary.

My manna from Heaven today:

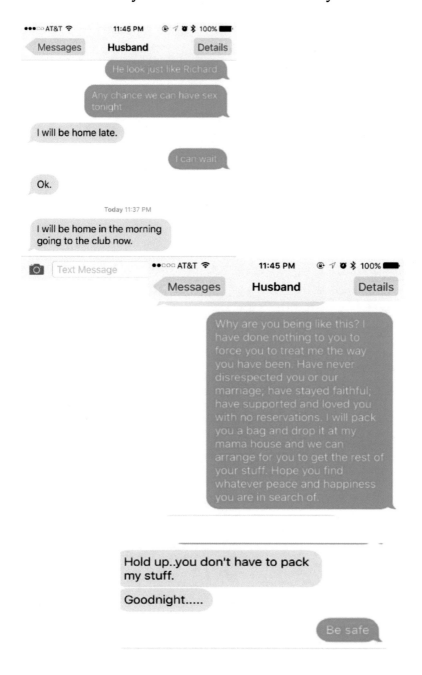

August 8, 2016

I had to cry out and worship before God my heart has been so heavy. I promise, though, God is an able God and is so marvelous and full of miracles. I didn't think I would be able to bear the pain I was in, but, because He is God He sustained me. My car quit on me in the middle of traffic today but, again, God being God had it all under control. I will delight in Him for He is my reward. I am starting a 40-day fast today.

My manna from Heaven today:

2 Timothy 1:7-8: For God hath not given us the spirit of fear; but of power, and of love, and of a sound mind. Be not thou therefore ashamed of the testimony of our Lord, nor of me his prisoner: but be thou partaker of the afflictions of the gospel according to the power of God.

If they took back the pain they caused, you'd lose the strength you gained.
- Rachel Wolchin

"

Today is a new day. A New opportunity to get better stronger faster smarter and closer to your goals and dreams. Take it.

Joel Madden

August 9, 2016

God is moving and I have resolved within myself to move with Him and not forget His presence nor His will. Tonight is Uncle Willie's wake. I asked Gary if he wanted to ride together (thinking for sure I was going to get the same response I have been getting; which has been no) well he shocked me because he said yes. Ok. Color me surprised.

My manna from Heaven today:

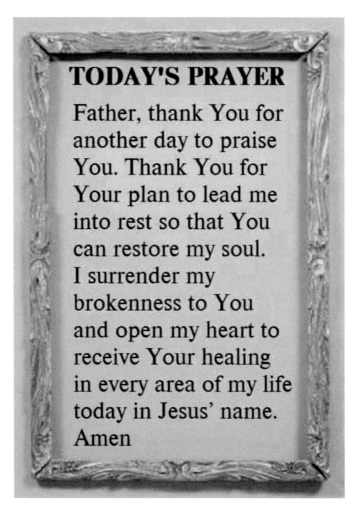

TODAY'S PRAYER

Father, thank You for another day to praise You. Thank You for Your plan to lead me into rest so that You can restore my soul. I surrender my brokenness to You and open my heart to receive Your healing in every area of my life today in Jesus' name. Amen

August 10, 2016

We buried Uncle Willie today. Gary is doing good. His grandmother is having a hard time. Praying for her strength. God is moving and He is the strength that we need. Man, I am preparing to cross the Jordan. I am standing on the edge right now, what am I going do? Stay encouraged.

Limitations live only in our minds.
But if we use our imaginations, our
possibilities become limitless.

Jamie Paolinetti

My manna from Heaven today:

Ephesians 1:18-19
[18] The eyes of your understanding being enlightened; that ye may know what is the hope of his calling, and what the riches of the glory of his inheritance in the saints, And what is the exceeding greatness of his power to us-ward who believe, according to the working of his mighty power.

Examined my life..I don't look like
what I am going through.

August 11, 2016

The Lord woke me up in the most special of ways today and invited me into His presence. He literally whispered, let's go to the garden!! I smile when I think about it, because He just didn't have to let me in. I am just saying, being in the presence of God is the most special thing. Started my small vacation today. I am not going anywhere, but I am in need of a break. I don't think I have ever been this tired before in my life. My soul is exhausted. But the joy of the Lord is my strength. In him, I find rest.

"

When you want something you've never had, you have to do something you've never done.

Unknown

My manna from Heaven today:

> Anyone can give up, it's the easiest thing in the world to do. But to hold it together when everyone else would understand if you fell apart, that's true strength.

Doing the right thing causes us to stand taller, dance more often, and step into life with more confidence.

Patsy Clairmont

August 12, 2016

Day two of my vacation and I have kids!! Gary and his dad are at the hospital with his Aunt Doris (who is doing better). His other aunt tried to kill herself today. I would ask when will it stop, but now, I just say thank you. God is moving and this is why I am in prayer. I thank God for what he is doing. Life still goes on, Lord teach me how to do so as well in You.

My manna from Heaven today:

Romans 8:37: In all things we are more than conquerors through him who loved us.

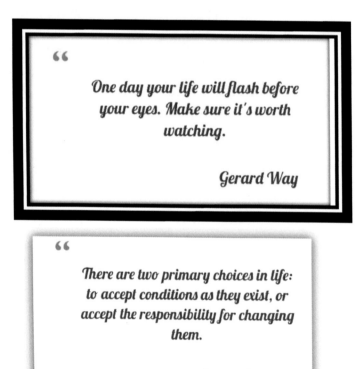

> One day your life will flash before your eyes. Make sure it's worth watching.
>
> Gerard Way

> There are two primary choices in life: to accept conditions as they exist, or accept the responsibility for changing them.
>
> Denis Waitley

August 13, 2016

Saturday morning, I want nothing more than to sleep in, but I have been called into a higher purpose. My sleeping days are over! The enemy declared war on my life, so I have to press even harder. I was in prayer at 4:30 a.m. anointing my house. All my babies are here too. Yes, they were all anointed as well. Nothing that isn't of God is staying in my home. The Lord is changing Gary in small ways, I can see it. I wonder does he recognize God's power in his life. Lord, open his eyes when the time is right. I spent all day at the waterpark with the church and the kids. TIRED!!

My manna from Heaven today:

I Corinthians 10:31
Whether you eat or drink, or whatever you do,
do all to the glory of God.

At Hurricane Harbor with the kids. This girl
right here, wore me out but I love, love, love
her! She gives me hope.
Aspen Kohl 2016

August 14, 2016

I spent the entire morning in worship. It has been a breathtaking week. Spending every morning in worship with God is refreshing. He just reveals, reveals, reveals. The heart of a worshipper. Gary has been with his dad at the hospital. He said he hasn't had a drink so that is really good. There is power in the Blood!!

My manna from Heaven today:

A quiet morning with a loving God puts the events of the upcoming day into proper perspective.

Jannette Oke

Looking unto Jesus the author and finisher of our faith; who for the joy that was set before him endured the cross, despising the shame, and is set down at the right hand of the throne of God. Hebrews 12:2

August 15, 2016

You can see the change! That was the word from God today. I am enjoying what little time off I have. Just being refreshed in God. Gary cried and tossed and turned in his sleep all night. His heart is so heavy, but I know God is moving. You can see the slow transformation of him back to himself. God is his strength. I anoint him everyday and our house and our bedroom. I am covering my whole house.

My manna from Heaven today:

Daniel 12:3: Those who are wise will shine like the brightness of the heavens.

This is what the situation started out looking like.

This is the end result!

No matter what happens stay in the fire!!!

August 16, 2016

I don't even know what day of my fast I am on. I am just so excited about what God is doing. Will I stand? That was the question he asked me today. Will I be one of the 3? I do not want to compromise the word of God in my life and be like the world. So many people are walking out on their marriages, but I thank God for staying power, even when I feel like I am looking like a fool. God you are so holy. That great hair style I had yesterday is completely gone. The rain is here. God has shown up. Lol

Casting all your care upon him, for he careth
for you. 1 Peter 5:7

My manna from Heaven today:

The day the rain came.

August 17, 2016

I am enjoying my time off. Seems like there is something to do every day. But I am enjoying the down time. I woke this morning in a place of worship and received an anointing word from the Lord. I am no longer dating God, I have married him. We are in a committed and dedicated relationship. I think back over the past few months when I have been tempted to change things in my own marriage, God has continued to remind me of dedication and commitment. I realize you can't be committed to anything or anyone unless you are first committed to God, because He is the one that keeps you.

My manna from Heaven today:

My babies. They take all my money, but these little people give me life.

It is the Lord's mercies that we are not consumed, because his compassions fail not. They are new every morning: great is thy faithfulness. Lamentations 3:22-23

August 18, 2016

I was supposed to go back to work today. I will admit I got up, then laid back down, then went in for a few hours, then came back home. I am just not ready to leave this place of rest yet, so since there is nothing pressing, I am going to enjoy.

My manna from Heaven today:

Back to bed!!

August 19, 2016

It is Friday and again wow to God!! After prayer I don't think I move for a few hours, but I had to get up and go to the grocery store. Movement is good, it lets you know there is still signs of life in you. I have really needed this refueling these past few days, but more importantly, I have needed the early morning prayer line. This fast has heaven written all over it. I am starting to remember my love for my husband. He is becoming a little more of himself again and I have really missed him. I thank God for preserving something to miss. I have got to start back exercising.

My manna from Heaven today:

Fight the urge to spread yourself too thin.
Hone in on what matters today.
Priscilla Shirer

August 20, 2016

"You have to learn to operate in love and forgiveness." Those were the words from God this morning. Love can change things. I am a witness! I went to a baby shower today. Praying that God moves on behalf of the young lady. Lord Your plan, Your move, Your will. We can't always see, but I know it's perfect. So I pray you keep her. Give her strength of character and peace in her heart. Give her the strength to break the curses over her life. Teach her how to trust in You and in You alone.

My manna from Heaven today:

No matter what, I have got to keep moving!

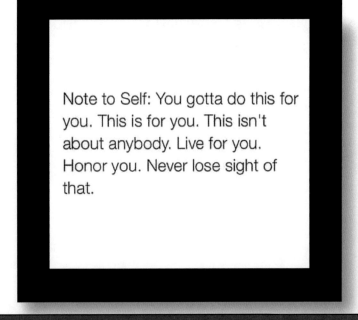

Note to Self: You gotta do this for you. This is for you. This isn't about anybody. Live for you. Honor you. Never lose sight of that.

Let your light shine before others, that they may see your good deeds and glorify your Father in heaven. Matthew 5:16

August 21, 2016

Joy, joy, joy lives in me today. Woke up this morning, my soul so overjoyed. I am watching Gary just come back to himself a little more every day. If I was not actually living it, I would not believe it was possible. There is no way anyone could make me understand this, if I was not seeing it with my own eyes. The power in which God is working cannot be contained.

My manna from Heaven today:

Blessed is the man whose strength is in thee; in whose heart are the ways of them. Who passing through the valley of Baca make it a well; the rain also filleth the pools. They go from strength to strength, every one of them in Zion appeareth before God. Psalms 84:5-7

August 22, 2016

The power and glory of God fell so hard yesterday during church. Who can compare to our God? I am starting to lose my voice. I shouted and worshipped so hard. Gary tapped me on my butt today. I know, it is such a small thing, but for me, where we are now in our relationship, it was gigantic! And he said "I haven't done that in a while." What!!! There is no one that can tell me God isn't faithful and can't change a situation. I did one of those silent screams and the happy dance, because that person is my husband, not this man who has been in my house!!

My manna from Heaven today:

You just have to keep pushing yourself.

God is moving and I have to keep going to!!

His divine power has given us everything we need for a godly life through our knowledge of him who called us by his own glory and goodness. 1 Peter 1:3

August 23, 2016

A heart full of gladness is what I have. Where I once had tears of sadness, God has turned them into joy. Gary even found something to smile about today. He isn't walking around the house brooding anymore like we all have the plague and he wants to get away from us. Only God could change that because I did everything I could. My God is faithful.

My manna from Heaven today:

I finally started back working out.

Never under estimate a woman with a prayer and a plan.

August 24, 2016

My soul makes a boast before the Lord. When I woke up this morning, my voice was completely gone. I finally went to the doctor; both of my ears are infected, I have laryngitis and a sinus infection. Who isn't being stopped is me. I've been walking around that sick and have felt nothing. A few months ago, well no, a month ago, I would have told you my husband didn't care, and the truth is he really wouldn't have. But like I said, he is coming back to himself. He took time out and picked up my medicine and made sure I was good. God is giving me back my love. I am looking at him and remembering why I love him; why I have been praying; why I have been fighting; why, even though I have tried, I can't let him go. He is a good man, no he is a great and mighty man. Not perfect, but truly good to his soul. God has greatness for him. Thank you Lord.

My manna from Heaven today:

Jeremiah 17:7-8: Blessed is the man that trusteth in the LORD, and whose hope the LORD is. For he shall be as a tree planted by the waters, and that spreadeth out her roots by the river, and shall not see when heat cometh, but her leaf shall be green; and shall not be careful in the year of drought, neither shall cease from yielding fruit.

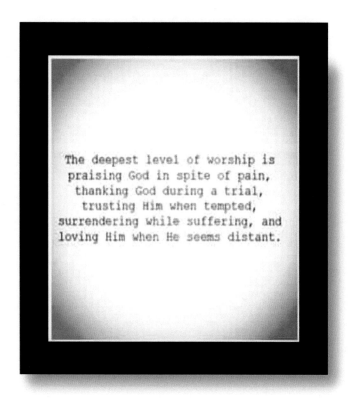

The deepest level of worship is praising God in spite of pain, thanking God during a trial, trusting Him when tempted, surrendering while suffering, and loving Him when He seems distant.

August 25, 2016

As I sit in this very spot, at this very moment, neither my soul nor my voice (for that matter) has words to describe how overjoyed my spirit is. God is moving in my life and He is restoring and there is no doubt that it is going to be even better than before, if that is even possible. God is giving my husband his mind back and I am so grateful I can't contain it. And to prove I am not crazy, Nicole is even noticing the difference. I am so full of praise. I didn't even know I had this level.

My manna from Heaven today:

Up and in prayer at 4:30 this morning, I guess I didn't need anything else!!

August 26, 2016

God is so magnificent. If anyone can find something greater let me know. Even when things are going bad, he is still God. God called Gary this morning and believe it or not he answered the call. He had to acknowledge the voice of God. He never wakes when I am in prayer and worship, and this morning I wasn't even loud and he heard the worship from heaven. My God is holy!!

My manna from Heaven today:

My birthday party! Summit Gym rock climbing. I made it to the top!! Happy dance!! Stronger than I was this time last year. I couldn't even make it half way the year before.

August 27, 2016

When you have had the year I have had to endure you really don't think that your birthday will be anything special. But I woke covered and wrapped in the spirit of God this morning. God rained down sweet presents from heaven for my birthday and the greatest one of all was restoring my husband's mind. I am so humbled and I feel so loved. There are no words, honestly. Today has been so great. So worth the fight. Worth the tears and worth the heartache. To experience the love of God like this, again no words!

My manna from Heaven today:

August 28, 2016

Just finished the prayer line and I feel drunk in the spirit. I didn't think I had the capacity to receive anything else. I am already overflowing but my cup keeps running over. Gary called last night to say he was going to the club and would be staying with his cousin for the night. I could have tripped but I choose instead to rejoice in the fact that he at least called to make sure that I was okay with it. I have to learn to trust again. God is showing me how to forgive with love.

My manna from Heaven today:

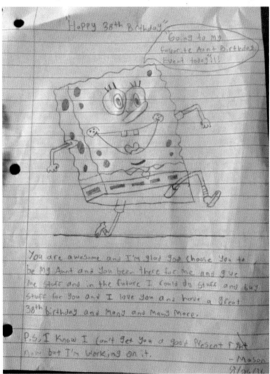

This is why I press.

August 29, 2016

Woke up before the alarm this morning just in a place of worship. Just so amazing to be in the presence of the Lord. Prayer was so good. I swear I could see a cloud just surrounding me while I was in worship. The spirit was running so through me I had to get up and go work out. I have the power to possess good health and I claim that power in the name of Jesus.

My manna from Heaven today:

This is why I can't quit. This is why I can't lose my peace. Even when it seems hopeless. I have got to keep pressing for them.

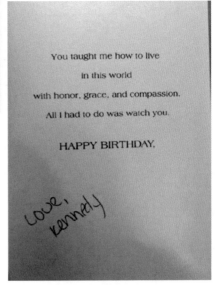

You taught me how to live

in this world

with honor, grace, and compassion.

All I had to do was watch you.

HAPPY BIRTHDAY,

love,
kennedy

August 30, 2016

Wake up the word! That was the word this morning on the prayer line. Sex is starting to happen a little more between me and Gary. We had sex twice this month. Huge improvement from where we started this year! I anointed our bed again this morning because the enemy is trying but he is not taking our passion and attraction for each other. I asked God for my own deliverance at the beginning of this year and I know that if I stay faithful he will give me just what I asked.

My manna from Heaven today:

Out of His fullness we have all received grace in place of grace already given. John 1:16

August 31, 2016

Worshipping Wednesday. Such a beautiful day to worship God. Worshipping him in all of His glory in the beauty of His holiness for God is worthy. Gary is doing well. Laughing, talking, playing. It is a little foreign to me now so much so, that I have to catch myself because I just sit and watch in amazement. A lot of thoughts are rolling thru my brain.

My manna from Heaven today:

> # The Lord will be your confidence and will keep your foot from being caught.
> # Proverbs 3:26

September 1, 2016

"Change your perception." That is the word that came from God on this morning. It is not what it looks like. How many times did God say that to me over the past 7 months. It is not what it looks like. September = Transformation and in Latin it means 7 and spiritually 7 represents completion. I have walked in complete transformation this month.

That was my manna from Heaven today

September 2, 2016

"Your suffering was for a purpose!" To shine bright like a diamond, I have to go through so God can cut some things off and shape me to be priceless. I love God because I can call him a friend. He reveals his plans to me. He doesn't leave me hopeless. He encourages me. He has taught me how to endure. I love him for that. Gary called from the road to let me know he had left town for a football game. I could have gotten upset but I chose instead once again to stay in a place of peace and joy. God is going to work everything out.

That was my manna from Heaven today

September 3, 2016

"Prophesied over yourself" was the word today. What am I speaking. I am in my feelings today. The enemy was trying to mess with my mind, but I put the word on him. It is written!! And it worked, God came and comforted me after. Can't help but serve him. Gary left for Austin yesterday for a football game. I had no knowledge he was going until he called me from the road to say he was gone. I haven't heard from him at all today. Again, I chose to stay in a place of peace and joy. It will all work out.

My manna from Heaven today:

I have set the LORD always before me: because he is at my
right hand,
I shall not be moved. Psalm 16:8

September 4, 2016

Remember the Lord thou God. Thank you Lord, for your goodness and mercy. Even in it all, God is good. Gary left on Friday heading to Austin for a football game didn't tell me until he was on his way. He didn't come home last night. I haven't heard from him at all. Nevertheless, I am encouraged. God is up to something even bigger in my life. It is hard to see, even harder to comprehend, but that is where I activate my faith and keep going.

My manna from Heaven today:

Psalm 63:1 O God, thou art my God; early will I seek thee: my soul thirsteth for thee, my flesh longeth for thee in a dry and thirsty land, where no water is;

September 5, 2016

"Stay steadfast." That is what He told me today. To be steadfast is to be unmovable; trusting, firm, planted, rooted. I have nothing else. Another night Gary didn't come home and didn't call and he isn't answering his phone. I promised myself a few weeks ago that if he did this again I was going to go ahead and pack his stuff. I really didn't think I would have to stand by those words. But, I did. I packed his clothes. This is not easy, but all God keeps saying is, "be steadfast." How do I do that when life is closing in on me?? The truth is I don't have anywhere else to go or anything else to do. He is all I have known. Almost 20 years together has come to this. As I sit on the floor crying tears I didn't know I had in me, God said it's all working for my good. The promises of God are everlasting.

My manna from Heaven today:

LIFE ISN'T ABOUT HOW TO SURVIVE THE STORM; IT'S ABOUT HOW TO DANCE IN THE RAIN.

September 6, 2016

Fifteen years of marriage and he didn't argue, didn't debate, didn't talk, didn't even put up a fight. He just loaded his stuff in the car and blamed me. How I am making it through today I have no clue. It hurts to blink, so I'll talk tomorrow.

September 7, 2016

I understand why Peter began to sink when he took his eyes off God. Told God yesterday I can't take my eyes from Him or I was going to be overtaken. "Be steadfast." Yesterday was hard. Today is much better. Today the sun is shining. It's all working for my good.

My manna from Heaven today:

Madeleine L'Engle: "Faith is what makes life bearable, with all its tragedies and ambiguities and sudden, startling joys."

---

1 Peter 1:8-9

Though you have not seen him, you love him; and even though you do not see him now, you believe in him and are filled with an inexpressible and glorious joy, for you are receiving the end result of your faith, the salvation of your souls.

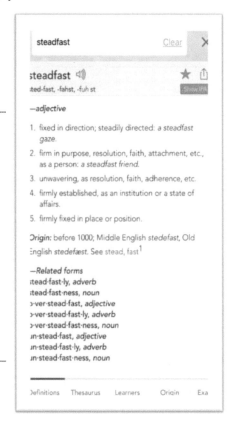

September 8, 2016

God is so good. Life is a little overwhelming right now, but I am encouraged. He is working all things together. My heart hurts and I mean it hurts bad. I can't focus. Gary claims all my thoughts but still I refuse to doubt God. It's working. I can't see it, but it's working. I can't feel it, but it's working. Walk in His ways, do good always and he will give me the fat of the land!! Abundance, even in pain.

My manna from Heaven today:

Trust in the Lord and do good; dwell in the land enjoy safe pasture. Psalm 37:3

September 9, 2016

I have been preparing for it and today it's finally here. Family reunion weekend!!! I have so much to do. Gary said he was coming, now he isn't. The joy of the Lord IS my strength.

My manna from Heaven today:

RULE FOR A
RELATIONSHIP

A man must take care
of his woman and a woman
must take care of her man.
No one is before the other.
It's about teamwork.
(Type "yes" if you agree)

*Don't be dejected and sad, for the joy of the
Lord is your strength. Nehemiah 8:10 NLT*

September 10, 2016

Lord God, what a day!! God is so wonderful. There are people that love and appreciate me. God gets all the glory because none of it was possible without him.

Colossians 3:17: Whatever you do, whether in word or deed, do it all in the name of the Lord Jesus, giving thanks to God and the Father by him.

My manna from Heaven today:

Renee Swope: "A woman with a confident heart chooses to believe that God wants to make an impact through her life and she looks for ways to let Him."

September 11, 2016

The family reunion ended today. It was amazing. All of the hard work and planning I have been doing this year was so worth it. We had an amazing time. Such a beautiful resort. I realized today, I was so busy this weekend that I didn't think about Gary at all and it was wonderful. Of course, now that I am on my way home he is plaguing my thoughts, and sadness is trying to make it's way back in. He was at the house this weekend, I can see hints of him. I just knew the car with his clothes was going to be gone but it is still there. Part of me is glad, the other part I don't know.

My manna from Heaven today:

Millcreek Ranch Resort, Canton Texas

September 12, 2016

Today isn't one of the best of days. Preparing to come off my fast, and the word from God was: "Don't rebuild what God has destroyed!" My strength was weak today, but I thank God he is still moving. I asked Gary if he was coming home anytime soon and he said no. I was upset, and bitterness and deep anger was trying to take root in me, but I am really learning to worship instead. I do not want anger and bitterness to make me miss my blessings. So instead of anger and sadness, I am going to continue to pray for him, and give him his space and when thoughts of him come to my mind, I will worship until they pass. God has him now.

My manna from Heaven today:

Ephesians 6:10 Be strong in the Lord and the power of his might.

All I have right now…

Book Two
All You Have to Do Is Get Up
Coming soon…

Afterword

My letters to God…

August 6, 2016

Lord where you lead I will follow. I will submit myself to you for you are my shield and my great reward. You light my feet, you guide me, you give me strength when I am weak. When I feel all hope is gone, you lift me up. When my heart is heavy, as it continues to be, you direct me. You are my God, my Keeper and my Guide. My soul makes a boast in you. I can't move without you. You watch me and keep me. My heart longeth after you. Even in my trials and tribulations I find strength in you. You are water to me; the very source of my life. You stretch me and refuse to let me fall. You love me even when I think there is nothing to love. You see me when no one else does. You remind me of this, when my heart is hurting, and I just want to forget. You always make me smile even when tears are rolling down my face, as they are right now. Who am I that you are mindful of me or that you remember such a low person as me. When things seem as if they are too hard to handle, you are there. When people that I love and trust misuse me and turn their backs on me, you are there. There is nowhere I can go that you won't find me. You feed me manna from heaven every day. No good or wonderful thing have you withheld from me. When I needed love in the physical you sent me Gary. He has made me laugh and although lately he makes me cry, you still remind me you selected him for me. You will not let us fall. Though we stumble you, are my Rock and my salvation. You gave me a mother that loves me. You made me fruitful and in you, Lord, there are no regrets. You have broken curses from off my life, you have taught me how to love and accept myself. I can search forever but there is none like you.

Shawnte

August 7, 2016

You ask me all the time now, what does love looks like to me? I thought I knew. In fact, I was 100% sure I knew because I thought I had it face to face with me every day. I really thought what we had was a real reflection of love. But I now know that that was one small piece in a much greater picture. Love is loyal; love is patient; love really is kind. I thought I understood that scripture and while it is easy to quote, I now know it's harder to live, and even harder to give. Love is long-suffering. Love is staying up late at night just to make sure he makes it home safely. Love is caring. It is listening even when your heart is heavy and breaking.

It doesn't take a count of all the things that you have done for each other. Love is pure. There are no strings attached. Love is keeping your mouth shut when all you want to do is scream, but instead knowing when and how to speak. Love is compromise. Love is about finding middle ground during a dispute. Love is gentle. Love never seeks to cause the recipient pain. Love is understanding. It gives him time and space that he needs to work through his internal struggles. Love is encouraging. It sends words to help uplift instead of tearing him down. Love cries sometimes, but love remembers. Love remembers better days, stronger days. Love remembers smiles and walks and passion and kissing and laughing and fighting and making up. Love remembers what love looks like. Love is faithful and allows nothing to separate it. Love is communication. Love is forgiveness. Real love never let go. You have challenged me Lord the last few months to really get to know what a real and true love looks like. More than that, you have challenged me to love who you gave me like that. I don't know if it is enough, but I do know that it is real. Please keep him safe. He is lost inside his head.

Please don't let him fall. He has so much strength, he has so much good in him. His smile is healing. His humor is infectious. His hands are strong. His heart is really real. His hugs make a bad day better and his wisdom is refreshing. His pride and his pain have a strong hold of him right now, but please don't allow him to destroy what you have built within him. Please Lord don't give up on him. His heart hurts. It has for a long time and believe me I know he is selfish, but he is worth it to your kingdom. Make him stronger than his pain, sorrow and anger. Me, I don't know anything else to do but to stand. Quitting isn't an option and you have me tied too strong to this life for me to leave. So, I have no choice but to stand. You said you wouldn't leave me. Lord, I don't want to be all high and holy, I only want to be beneficial. I only want to be in your will because I want to walk this life in abundance. You promised me so many things, but never did I anticipate the cost. I will gladly pay it. You said what used to work isn't going to work anymore. Show me what you need. I asked for abundance and I am serious about it. I don't know how to function at the level that I am at today. My tears are my only comfort right now. I am so confused and brokenhearted, but I am grateful that you comfort the brokenhearted.

Shawnte

September 3, 2016

You have been talking to me all day. Your voice is so clear in my head and your presence is so real in my heart. But it still doesn't stop the pain, or the feeling of loneliness and emptiness. It doesn't stop the feeling of neglect and my mind has tried so hard to dwell on those emotions today. Anger and betrayal and bitterness has been working hard to try to set in, but you won't allow it. Your word has taken root in my life, Lord. Why can't everyone love me like you do? Why can't the men in my life love me and want me like you do? Am I that hard to love? I know I have given you trouble, and I know I am not easy to deal with, but you still love me. It is funny, the men that don't have to love me love me so much and yet the ones who are supposed to love me can't handle the job. First my father and now my husband. I would think it was me if I hadn't stopped and looked around. You still love me. It is comforting, but God between me and you, right now it doesn't feel like it is enough. My heart actually hurts. The pain will not stop the tears won't stop. It hurts. Yet at the same time it doesn't. It is crazy, I know, and I can't explain it except to say I have truly woken up to the Word and I have peace in my storm. No things are not what they look like and you are changing him. Things will not only get better, but it will be better than it was originally. There are promises on the other side of my heartache. That is why I can still smile, although I am in pain.

Shawnte

Made in the USA
Coppell, TX
28 March 2021

52586907R00081